I Heard

An American Journey

Jaha Nailah Avery

Illustrated by Steffi Walthall

Charlesbridge

Now listen, children, gather 'round,
and heed my every word.
I want to show you what I found
and tell you what . . .

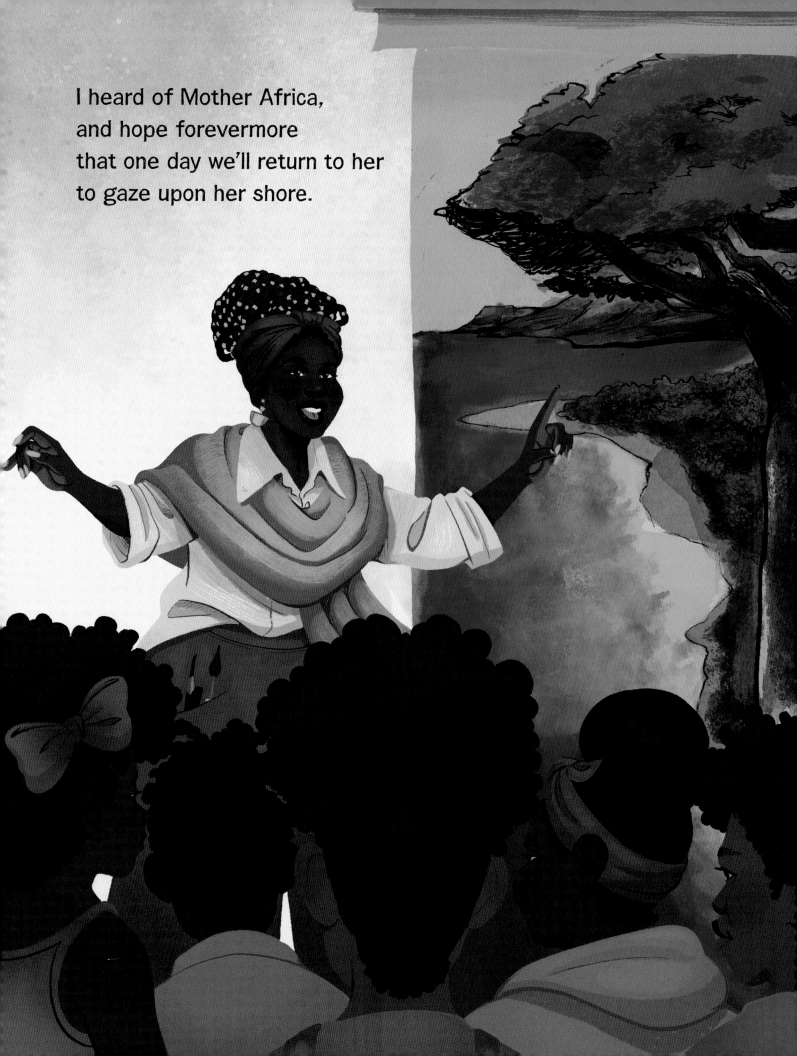

I heard of Mother Africa,
and hope forevermore
that one day we'll return to her
to gaze upon her shore.

I heard of hills and fields so lush
they make the old frog sing,
and birds so bright they make you blush,
and air as fresh as spring.

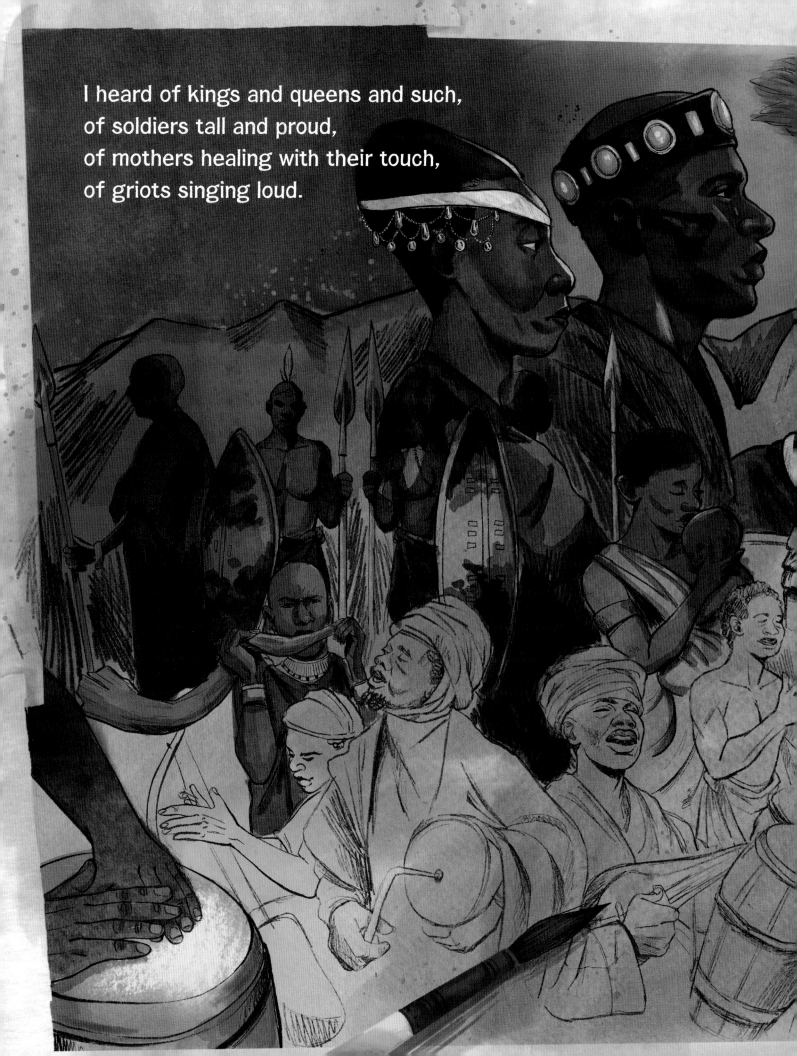

I heard of kings and queens and such,
of soldiers tall and proud,
of mothers healing with their touch,
of griots singing loud.

I heard the people, Black and free,
community abounds,
thus living all in harmony
with sky, with sea, with ground.

I heard about the great big ships
that crossed a bloody sea,
of shackled people in their grips,
all bound for slavery.

I heard about the auction block,
the whip, the prod, the chain,
the people branded like livestock,
the tears, the prayers, the pain.

I heard about the Underground,
the Railroad through the night,
the maps of moss the people found,
the North Star shining bright.

I heard about the drinking gourd.
The Freedom Train is boarding!
When "Moses" came, they thanked the Lord
and crossed the mighty Jordan.

I heard about the Civil War.
Black people proudly fought
for slavery to be no more
and liberation bought.

I heard of Reconstruction time,
when freedom had a chance.
But promises were nullified,
eight years, the same old dance.

I heard of crosses set ablaze,
of "strange fruit" in the tree,
of sharecropping and chain-gang days,
and testing lit'racy.

I heard of sit-ins, bus boycotts,
and countless demonstrations,
of protests rising, strong and hot,
displayed throughout the nation.

I heard of "freedom over me"
and "music in the air,"
"Lift Every Voice and Sing,"
a home promised "over there."

I heard about the riots' flames
and schools during segregation,
of HBCU football games,
and D9 org formation.

I heard about the major wars
and Black men who enlisted
to bravely fight across the shores,
though here no rights existed.

I heard of Freedom Riders and
the N-A-A-C-P.
The Green Book helped folks cross the land.
A preacher had a dream.

I heard of Panthers standing proud,
and SNCC forming at Shaw,
the Civil Rights Act ringing loud,
and changes in the law.

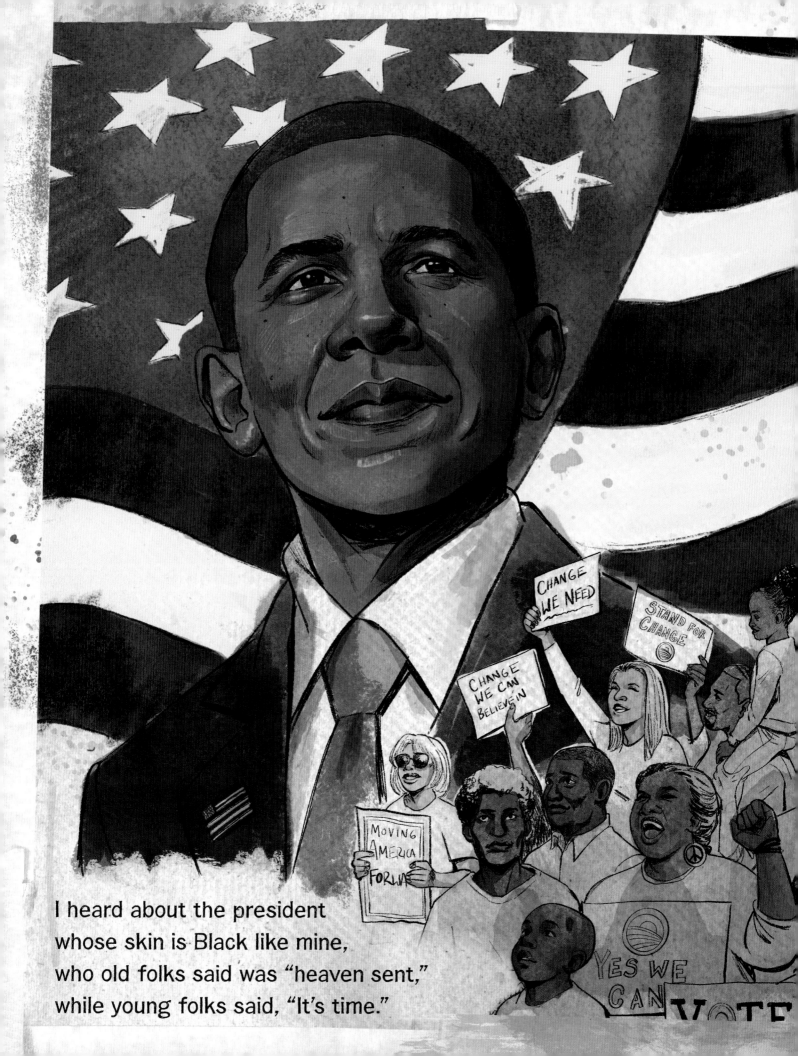

I heard about the president
whose skin is Black like mine,
who old folks said was "heaven sent,"
while young folks said, "It's time."

I heard of "Black Lives Matter" calls
and "defund the police."
I saw a gentle giant fall
and worldwide cries for peace.

I heard of unfair voter laws—
how fights against them grew.
How one woman took up the cause
and helped turn Georgia blue.

And up there on the highest court,
a new judge joined the action.
Black and brilliant, wise and short.
They call her JUSTICE Jackson.

So, children, that is what I heard,
but this is not the end.
Keep marching forward, undeterred.
Together, we will win!

And as you go about your day,
remember to think back
on all the ones who paved the way
and be proud to be Black!

LEARN MORE

Black Lives Matter: Black Lives Matter is a civil rights organization formed to protest injustices against Black people. Beyond the organization, "Black Lives Matter" is also a powerful statement of truth and a rallying cry for Black life to be cherished and valued.

Chain gang: This was an attempt to keep Black people stuck in a system similar to slavery. Black people would be arrested for made-up charges, then chained together and forced to work, often to death. The chain gangs built many of the rail systems, roads, and other infrastructure that we still use today.

Civil Rights Act: The Civil Rights Act of 1964 banned discrimination based on race, religion, and nationality in public places and schools.

D9: The Divine 9 is a group of nine elite Black fraternities and sororities, some of which have been in existence for over a century:
- Alpha Phi Alpha Fraternity, founded 1906, Cornell University
- Alpha Kappa Alpha Sorority, founded 1908, Howard University
- Kappa Alpha Psi Fraternity, founded 1911, Indiana University
- Omega Psi Phi Fraternity, founded 1911, Howard University
- Delta Sigma Theta Sorority, founded 1913, Howard University
- Phi Beta Sigma Fraternity, founded 1914, Howard University
- Zeta Phi Beta Sorority, founded 1920, Howard University
- Sigma Gamma Rho Sorority, founded 1922, Butler University
- Iota Phi Theta Fraternity, founded 1963, Morgan State University

Drinking gourd: The song "Follow the Drinking Gourd" is actually a code. It provided instructions to enslaved African Americans on how to escape slavery by following the Big Dipper and North Star, so they would always know which way was north to freedom. It could be sung in front of white people, who assumed that the song was about heaven.

Freedom Riders: The Freedom Riders were civil rights activists who organized bus rides into segregated states to protest segregation within the busing system. Freedom Riders' buses were often targeted, burned, and shot at, and many Freedom Riders were killed.

Gentle giant: George Floyd was affectionately referred to as a "gentle giant" by those who knew him. He was killed by police in May 2020, setting off worldwide protests against police brutality toward African Americans and all Black people.

Georgia turning blue: African American politician Stacey Abrams worked to "turn Georgia blue" in the 2020 presidential election, meaning that more Georgians voted for the Democratic candidate (blue) than the Republican candidate (red). Georgia had previously voted Republican in the presidential election for decades.

The Green Book: During the Jim Crow era, when laws supported racial segregation, Black people could only stay at certain hotels, eat at certain restaurants, and get gas at certain gas stations. *The Negro Motorist Green Book* was published every year as a guide for Black travelers to know where they could safely eat, shop, and rest while traveling.

Griots: Griots are the historians and storytellers in communities across the continent of Africa. They know the history of the people and the land, and they often include music in their storytelling.

HBCU: Historically Black Colleges and Universities started in the mid-1800s as a way to educate many formerly enslaved people, because Black people could not attend white schools for another century.

Jordan: Several Negro spirituals reference the River Jordan, where Jesus Christ was baptized. This was coded advice to go through every body of water possible when escaping slavery, as it would help throw the patrol dogs off your scent.

Justice Jackson: In April 2022, Judge Ketanji Brown Jackson was confirmed by the Senate as the first Black woman to serve as a justice on the United States Supreme Court.

"Lift Every Voice and Sing": This song is the African American (formerly "Negro") National Anthem, written by James Weldon Johnson in 1900.

Maps of moss: In the Northern Hemisphere, moss grows on the north side of trees. Enslaved African Americans who were planning to escape were often advised that moss would point them north toward freedom.

Moses: "Moses" was a nickname for Harriett Tubman, who led thousands of enslaved African Americans to freedom. In the biblical book of Exodus, Moses led the people of God out of slavery in Egypt.

NAACP: The National Association for the Advancement of Colored People (NAACP) is a civil rights organization formed in 1909 to fight for justice for African Americans. The NAACP was instrumental in securing and protecting voting rights, documenting and protesting lynchings, and supporting and enacting legislation that benefited African American communities. Today the NAACP addresses inequality in the criminal justice system, prison reform, economic opportunities, and much more for all Black people in America.

Negro spirituals: This is a group of hymns created and sung by enslaved African American people. These hymns include "Oh, Freedom," "I Hear Music in the Air," and "Jesus Promised Me a Home Over There."

Panthers: The Black Panther Party was a Black Power political organization formed in 1966 to protect and enrich Black communities. The Black Panthers documented and fought police brutality, introduced a Free Breakfast for Children program, and created community health clinics.

Preacher's dream: Dr. Martin Luther King, Jr. delivered his famous "I Have a Dream" speech at the March on Washington in 1963, when 250,000 people gathered to demand civil rights for African Americans.

President Barack Obama: Obama was elected the first Black President of the United States in 2008 and served two terms.

Sharecropping: Sharecropping was started to keep Black people in a system similar to slavery. Black farmers grew crops on farmland owned by white people for very little pay. The goal was to keep them in debt so they couldn't leave.

SNCC (pronounced "snick"): The Student Nonviolent Coordinating Committee (SNCC) was formed at Shaw University in 1960 by a group of African American college students. Hundreds of students came together to organize boycotts, sit-ins, and other nonviolent protests against discrimination.

Strange fruit: This refers to the dead bodies of African Americans who had been lynched and left hanging from trees. "Strange Fruit" started out as a poem by Abel Meeropol, published under his pen name, Lewis Allan. It was later famously recorded as a song by Billie Holiday.

Underground Railroad: The Underground Railroad was a network of secret routes established in the 1800s to help enslaved African Americans escape to freedom.

AMERICAN CIVIL RIGHTS ACTIVISTS
(from top left to bottom right)

Malcolm X – American Muslim minister and civil rights activist

Fannie Lou Hamer – American civil rights activist who battled for voting and economic rights

Shirley Chisholm – First African American woman in Congress; first woman to run for US president

Nina Simone – American singer, musician, and civil rights activist

Daisy Bates – American civil rights activist who reported on the battle to end segregation in Arkansas

Joyce Ladner – American civil rights activist; field secretary for SNCC

Diane Nash – American civil rights activist; cofounder of SNCC; guided Freedom Riders to Alabama

Medgar Evers – Southern civil rights activist; first NAACP field officer in Mississippi

Fred Hampton – American civil rights activist; deputy chairman of the Black Panther party

John Lewis – American civil rights activist and politician; chairman of SNCC

For my great-grandmothers, Katie Crews Watson and Lilora Rogers Avery.—J. N. A.

For Kingston, Levi, Jael, Charles D., and Lukas—proud of who you are & who you will be!—S. W.

AUTHOR'S NOTE

While in conversation with various people over the years, I realized that many believe the history of African Americans starts with slavery. This is not only false, but damaging and dangerous. It perpetuates the idea that the origin of African American culture is found in the belly of slave ships or on the auction blocks of old. But I ask this question: What are the things that can be taken, and what are the things that cannot? Our culture consists of our people, our communities, and our shared history, heritage, and traditions. Some things were kept, some have been reclaimed, and all have been protected.

I Heard started out as a single stanza that I wrote for a contest at my (then) workplace. I had just returned from a life-changing trip to West Africa and felt more deeply connected to my history and heritage as an African American woman than ever. Reflecting on my travels and the significance of my time in Ghana, I wrote:

> I heard of Mother Africa,
> and hope forevermore
> that one day we'll return to her
> to gaze upon her shore.

The work contest ended (I didn't win, by the way), but I kept thinking about the beauty and resilience of my community. Yes, slavery is a defining piece of our story, but it is far from the whole picture. The story of African Americans is also one of triumph, of joy, of community, of creativity, and of victory. We are here, and we have a rich, thriving culture forged in the face of some of the most brutal, oppressive conditions seen throughout human history. We have our own language (African American Vernacular English, or AAVE), schools, organizations, leaders, foods, artistic expression, and much more, and of that, we should all be very proud.

Reminding myself of all this, I took that single stanza and began to add to it. The more I thought about the journey we have taken as African Americans, the longer *I Heard* grew. In this work, I hoped to capture the fullness and richness of our experiences as a people, in both triumph and despair.

I have always loved the lyrics to the African American National Anthem, "Lift Every Voice and Sing." I remember learning the lyrics as a little girl, and even back then, I thought it was one of the most beautiful songs I had ever heard. Two of my favorite lines are "Sing a song full of the faith that the dark past has taught us. / Sing a song full of the hope that the present has brought us." This is my culture, and *I Heard* is my song. It is a tribute to the enduring heritage of African Americans and our lasting impact on this country and on the world. Thank you for reading.

Published by Charlesbridge
9 Galen Street, Watertown, MA 02472
(617) 926-0329 · www.charlesbridge.com

Printed in China
(hc) 10 9 8 7 6 5 4 3 2 1

Illustrations done in digital media
Text type set in Franklin Gothic Hand Light
Printed by 1010 Printing International Limited in Huizhou, Guangdong, China
Production supervision by Jennifer Most Delaney
Designed by Cathleen Schaad

Library of Congress Cataloging-in-Publication Data
Names: Avery, Jaha Nailah, author. | Walthal, Steffi, illustrator.
Title: I heard / Jaha Nailah Avery; illustrated by Steffi Walthal.
Description: Watertown, MA: Charlesbridge, [2024] | Audience: Ages 5–8. | Audience: Grades 2–3. | Summary: "This lyrical poem tells the story of Black History in America, from slavery to the Civil Rights movement to present day struggles." —Provided by publisher.
Identifiers: LCCN 2022060677 (print) | LCCN 2022060678 (ebook) | ISBN 9781623543822 (hardcover) | ISBN 9781632893598 (ebook)
Subjects: LCSH: Children's poetry, American. | African Americans—Juvenile poetry. | CYAC: African Americans—Poetry. | LCGFT: Poetry.
Classification: LCC PS3601.V4685 I15 2024 (print) | LCC PS3601.V4685 (ebook) | DDC 811/.6--dc23/eng/20230307
LC record available at https://lccn.loc.gov/2022060677
LC ebook record available at https://lccn.loc.gov/2022060678